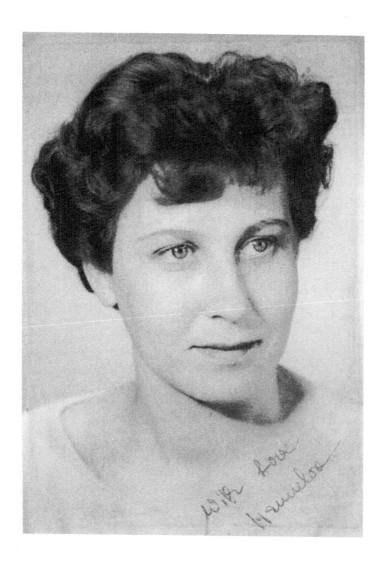

THE OTHER SIDE

THE MEMOIR OF A YOUNG GERMAN GIRL'S LIFE ON THE OTHER SIDE OF WAR

HANNELORE MACKENZIE

THE OTHER SIDE

First Published by Hannelore Mackenzie 2020

This book is dedicated to Mac, my family, my children and grandchildren, and to the memory of my parents.

Introduction.

Although urged by friends this has taken me years to write

It is all long ago now, and I think it is time we put the war behind us, and try to live together in peace. However, when I read books with misleading descriptions, I am absolutely stunned. For instance one book claimed a gentleman living in Berlin, was chauffeur driven to his office every morning, his servants used the second car, and his daughters, wearing, beautiful gowns, rushed from party to party, naturally also driven by the family chauffeur.

I once saw a film where people had a wonderful time going from party to party in taxis. Maybe high officials enjoyed parties, but the ordinary people didn't even know what a party was.

One writer described how utterly terrified she was of her husband because he was a German soldier. No doubt this sometimes happened. Most German soldiers were husbands, fathers, brothers and sons, ordinary men doing what they could to protect their family.

I read in some teaching material that German women had Hitler's picture in their houses because it was a talisman and kept them safe. No doubt, some deluded women did believe that. However, all German households had a Hitler picture because it was law.

Reading these items which seem to me to be far removed from the life of ordinary people, convinced me that it might be a good idea to write down what it was like for me and my family.

As the years go by memories fade and I feel that the facts are more and more distorted.

In this memoir I don't intend to dig too deeply into historical facts, many of which have been covered by many authors from every possible angle.

There is also a lot written about the Nazi terror. I am certain groups of people, the Jews, Communists, some religious groups, lived in terror, but the ordinary German population never felt terrorized by their leaders.

I'm writing down as much as I remember about what life was like during the war, because all these details will be lost once my generation dies out

Chapter One

'It's happened. War has been declared,' my mother said, and I was terrified. I stared out of the window across the back garden and the adjoining allotments to the main road.

Adults still talked about the horrors of World War I, and said if there ever were another war it would be even worse. And now there was another war. What would happen?

Would there be movement of military vehicles on the street I could see, with people shooting each other, or even fighting in our small lane? Would people shoot at us? The possibilities were too awful to consider. What, just what could anyone do?

We knew that we could do nothing to stop what was coming. The declaration of war was a fact one had to deal with.

The Kaisler family – my parents, Walter and Klara, my elder brother Horst, my younger sister Helga and me, Hannelore, recently moved into the downstairs flat of a small two family house situated in a short lane on the outskirts of Magdeburg, a town on the river Elbe. We had not even settled in properly when the disastrous news was announced.

I was eleven at the time, and it was the second time we had moved.

During the depression, and the period of German inflation, my father had lost his inheritance, a printing office. I remember my mother talking of those days.

'I rushed to the office every night to meet your father,' she said, 'and then we went as quickly as possible to the butcher, baker and grocer to buy a few things before the money was devalued even more.' A famous story of the time was that a basket with money was left outside a shop. The basket was stolen, but the money was left behind!

We had lost everything, leaving my father without a job, without an income. My father would put his hand to anything he could find to support his family.

Horst and I had not been aware of the crucial shortage of money, as my parents managed to keep life as normal as possible and provide us with sufficient, mainly with the help of my mother's parents.

My grandfather owned a wholesale grain business, in a town called Eilenburg, near Leipzig. Leipzig was the town where we had lived, and the place where my brother and I were born. Somehow his business had not greatly suffered in the inflation, or had recovered, I'm not sure which.

At the age of six I started school, and my parents managed to provide me with the traditional "Zuckertüte", or "sugar bag". This wonderful treat is a cone made from decorated cardboard; this "Zuckertüte" is filled with sweets, chocolate, biscuits, all to sweeten the first day at school. This tradition carries on today when parents collect their child from school on that very important first day and present them with their "Zuckertüte".

As my parents fought to stay on top, a friend offered my father a job in Mecklenbug, an area next to the Baltic Sea, and he accepted.

I was seven or eight at the time, and was still attending primary school and Horst had moved to the grammar school. German children did not wear school uniforms, but each grammar school had its own special cap, which was worn with pride.

It was a wrench for my parents to leave Leipzig where they lived all their lives, leaving family and friends behind. My brother very much regretted having to abandon his cap and change schools.

My mother's parents lived in Leipzig, my grandmother was disabled, and my mother often helped out.

My grandparents had a live-in maid, a girl who did not get paid much, but anybody with a job had free board and lodging, which counted for a lot in those days. My grandmother always had somebody with her even so my mother's help was often needed. It was hard for my mother to leave knowing she couldn't help anymore.

The distance between us was particularly distressing once war started. Girls who worked as home helps were called up, or worked in the factories to help the war effort.

In Leipzig we lived in the large flat where my father had been born, as were Horst and I. My parents took it over when my paternal grandparents died.

The death of my father's parents was a great tragedy, as they both died in the same week and were only in their fifties. When the facts were related to me I couldn't understand why everybody was so horrified. They had been over fifty, and in my mind that was old, very old, and of course old people died.

So the time had come for my father had to say good-bye to the only home he had ever known, which does not sound unusual now when people move quite frequently, but in those days people did not move as much.

The old flat in Leipzig was in a large corner house, on the third floor. In those days it was a small apartment, but now it would be called a place of generous proportions.

Living on the third floor meant it was difficult for me to go out alone to play, so my father fixed a swing in the huge hall, which was eleven metres long! The front room was an impressive nine metres. We had a playroom and a bedroom and there was my parents' bedroom, my father's study, kitchen and bathroom. We had been used to having plenty of living space, but now it had to be left behind.

'It won't be easy,' my mother said one day and sounded very sad, 'but it's got to be done.'

All of us, including the dog, crammed into my father's small Opel, and set out on a long journey to Waren, a small town on the shore of a lake called Müritz in the county of Mecklenburg.

Car journeys, in small cars, were far from comfortable in those days. Even so to own a car was a luxury. In our case the firm my father was going to work for had provided the car, as it was essential for the job. The German region called the Erzgebirge, is situated in the East, south of Leipzig, and was famous for producing beautiful wooden articles. One of my father's friends owned a firm, which made and sold these items, and wanted to extend their sales area. When I say they made the items, it is not quite correct. The company provided the materials and sold the goods, but home workers made them all.

My father's job was to visit schools in Mecklenburg and introduce a range of these wooden items, mainly beautifully carved Christmas decorations. I remember there were groups of angels playing instruments, delicate pyramids, picture frames, bowls, and much more. My father was to give talks about the history of the Erzgebirge home workers and the items they created.

The small car, which went with the job, didn't boast very soft springs, and as the roads in many areas were pretty rough, I felt often like I was being shaken like a cocktail, although I don't believe the expression cocktail was known in Germany in those days. There was no heating, and a winter journey meant wearing everything warm one could lay one's hands on, and cover oneself with blankets, except for my father who could not afford to be covered in blankets and had to depend on warm shoes and several layers of socks.

The journey was long, and eventually we arrived at our new town. At first we stayed in temporary accommodation, before we moved into a house with a garden. A garden was something exciting to us city dwellers, and was greatly appreciated by our Airedale Terrier. The dog had been a present from the breeder, a friend of my father's. Looking back, I wonder how we managed to afford to feed the dog, as we could barely afford to feed ourselves.

It only took a few days for the dog to meet his arch enemy. A middle sized grey dog which regularly walked along the road, stopped at our house, and barked his head off. At that sound our dog rushed to one of the front windows and joined the barking. The noise was deafening, and no doubt, an absolute delight for the neighbours!

Waren was a charming place, and we enjoyed living there. We often crossed the lake by boat, or if my father could spare the time, he drove us right round the lake, and we spent lovely days at the shore. We played in the lake, and screamed like mad when a water snake appeared, we reached top swimming speeds when trying to get out of its way.

If we made the trip by car, we would gather mushrooms on our return journey in the meadow between the lake and a small wood. We also collected fir cones in the woods, which were used as fuel for the kitchen stoves of the time. So on our outing we acquired supper and the means to cook it.

Horst joined the local grammar school, but I could not attend till I was ten. When I was nine, my teachers told my parents that, if they wished, I could sit the entry examination for the grammar school that year. And that is what I did. My father took me to the school and told me that he would collect me at the end of the day.

The day started with written exams, followed by oral tests for pupils who had not done well enough in the written work. Obviously my results were good enough because I didn't have to take the orals.

The afternoon was taken up by extensive sports activities, as the leaders of the Third Reich were very keen on sport.

At the end of the day my father came back for me, and I clearly remember that he produced a chocolate bunny in silver wrapping, and it dawned on me that I must have passed the entry exam.

At that time we enjoyed an addition to the family when Helga was born in 1937.

After passing the entry exam I started to attend grammar school at Easter, which was the time all German children started school. This particular establishment was a lovely small place, which only had between 12 or 14 pupils in each form, boys and girls together. My form consisted of 10 boys and 4 girls.

One of the pupils was a pretty and clever Jewish girl whose parents owned a Gentleman's outfitters. I can vaguely picture the shop and her friendly parents. Her sister was in fact the poor girl who joined an all boys' class, and the third child, a boy, was blond and blue-eyed.

As I said, sport was an important item at the time. So once a week, before lessons started, our sports teacher took us to a little pier by the lake, and taught us diving. He threw coins into the clear water, and we had to dive to retrieve them. Sometimes we saw an old gentleman who swam every day of the year.

I had become friendly with the Jewish girl, and we visited each other, but in early 1937 my mother said one day,

'You mustn't go to see the Jewish family anymore.'

'Why not?' I asked, confused why I could not go and see my friend.

'I don't really know,' she said, 'but we are not supposed to visit Jewish families anymore.'

As it happened I didn't get the chance to see them again because the family moved away. I don't know what happened to them, but I sincerely hope they emigrated.

My parents were friendly with a couple that owned a restaurant with a ballroom with a cinema attached. The residents of the town were quite excited when a film star of the time could, from time to time, be seen in the cinema when she came to visit her sister who lived in the area. The cinema offered a pleasant entertainment, and we enjoyed watching many films

The restaurant was a lucrative business although perhaps not the most elegant. Saturday dances tended to get rather noisy when a number of women Arbeitsdienst members met soldiers of an Army unit, who were stationed nearby. Literally translated Arbeitsdienst means 'workers duty'. Those units were created in 1935 to counteract unemployment, and stated that young men between 18 and 26 had to serve 6 months in the Arbeitsdienst to carry out necessary work. Of course, when war started, young men joined the Armed Forces without serving in the Arbeitsdienst.

It was while we were living in Waren that I saw Hitler in person. He was being driven in an open car through the streets, which were lined with people shouting 'Heil'.

I have no idea if they were all Hitler supporters, but as nobody forced them to stand and shout, one must imagine they were. It should be said that when Winston Churchill, no doubt Germany's enemy number one, visited Germany after the war, people cheered him as well. So perhaps people simply like to shout and cheer.

Chapter Two

I imagine that somehow my father's job did not work out properly, or maybe he got a better offer, but we left the small town.

There were five of us crammed into the car, complete with dog, of course. It was a long journey to Magdeburg, a town on the river Elbe. My father started his new civil service job, and my Horst and I joined new schools.

My father's office was in one of the buildings surrounding the cathedral square, with the impressive cathedral in the middle.

As we had come from a small place to a big city, my parents were advised to place me in a Mittelschule (a school taking pupils to the equivalent of our GCSE level) rather than trying to catch up with the standards of the town's grammar school. My parents took their advice, which we regretted. To try and resolve this, we applied to a grammar school.

My mother and I went along for an interview, and it emerged that I would have been accepted had I been willing to lose one or two years, which I was not. I was very proud of the fact that I started secondary education a year earlier than usual, and was not prepared to fall behind. As it turned out, I hadn't lost anything. Grammar school pupils had to leave the school before they could to sit the final examination, instead they had to take an emergency exam, meaning they had to catch up after the war.

So I stayed at the Mittelschule. Getting there involved a long walk or bicycle ride, as school buses were not available in those days. I was not exactly unhappy at the new school, but badly missed the school I had just left. The new place made little impression on me, nor did I have any special school friends, but I can still picture the form mistress. She was a fierce looking lady with spectacles toppling on the end of her nose. She taught French and did not stand for any nonsense, unlike one of the teachers at my previous school, who repeatedly stated that he'd prefer to work in a stone quarry than trying to teach us French.

At my other school it was taken for granted that boys were better pupils.

'Come on, boys,' the teachers would say,' you can't let the girls be better than you.'

This would give the boys added incentive to do their best, but although we girls had never heard of equal rights for men and women, we did not want to be outdone by the boys, and therefore everybody tried their hardest.

I had left all that behind me and had to get used to my new school.

I was 11 years old at the time, and we lived in a small ground floor flat of a two family house. The owners of the property occupied the upstairs flat. There were several small and simple houses in the short lane situated in the outskirts of Magdeburg. These small houses provided accommodation for the owners, with a second flat rented out to cover the costs. This was often the only way of owning a property in Germany, and even this was rare. Usually only the richest of the rich could afford to own houses.

The majority of people lived in rented accommodation, which ranged from primitive flats in Hinterhäuser, to high luxury apartments. Hinterhäuser (back houses) were a row of houses built in the back yards of the properties facing the street, where the poor lived, and one did not talk to people who lived in those houses.

I started school with a girl who lived in the house behind ours. As we went to school together it was quite natural that we saw each other at home. I even went shopping with the girl once, and my mother was horrified when she found out that I had been to a Co-operative Shop.

Before the war we did not shop at this Co-op's, however, all that was in the past, and we hadn't properly settled in our new home when the war started.

The beginning of the war didn't bring any drastic changes to our daily lives. All men of a certain age were called up, but as my father was too old for active service, and my brother too young, we were not personally involved.

My mother was extremely thankful for the fact that Horst, 15 at the time, was too young to be called up, and as everybody knew the war would be over in no time at all, there was no danger that he would have to join the forces.

Many women could not see why anyone should fight at all.

'Why not lock the leaders in a room and let them fight it out without involving the people?' they would say.

As well as the long walk to school we also had to walk to the weekly Hitler Youth meetings. The Jungmädel was the first stage of the female Hitler youth which one joined at the age of 10. So in 1939 I must have been a member, but I can't recall when and where I joined, have long since forgotten where we met, and have only the vaguest memory of what happened at those meetings. Clearly they did not make a big impression on me. The uniform we wore at that stage was a dress with a brown top and striped skirt, but I wouldn't swear to it.

I do remember on one occasion when a group of girls visited a military hospital to cheer up the wounded soldiers, which I do not think was a very clever idea. We were led into the cellar of the hospital where the wards for severely wounded soldiers were. The wards were in the cellar so the patients did not have to be moved during air raids. I remember being extremely frightened when I saw these horribly injured young men, and crept silently past their beds. I doubt that seeing a bunch of children was of any consolation to them.

When I said our daily life was not markedly changed at the beginning of the war, I must point out that the ration cards were introduced straight away. At that time the meat ration for a month was only 1.5 kilo.

One thing stuck in my mind very clearly all those years, namely the first item of food, which disappeared from the shelves. It was a Fünferstück, a weekly treat my mother bought from the baker. Called Fünferstück because it cost fünf (five) Pfennig, and it was a very large Danish pastry.

Although my father didn't work for the company who had provided the car, they gave the car to him. Unfortunately, at the beginning of the war there was no petrol allowance given to ordinary people whatsoever, and large cars were 'called up' for military use. We could not use the car anymore, and my father put it up on wooden blocks.

My memory of the time is perhaps fainter as one might expect, but as we had moved a lot, my pictures of places and events were not very strong. At that stage my Horst had reached the age where he was due to be confirmed.

As anything religious was not frowned upon, he attended a 'Jugendweihe' (Youth Consecration). It was a ceremony much like a confirmation but not carried out by a priest in church. My father could not get the time off to attend, so my mother, my little sister and I were present, It was an unremarkable affair and passed without leaving a great impression on me. I can't even recall that there had been a celebration, as one would expect at a church confirmation.

A few houses along our lane lived a young woman whose husband had been called up, and as she was expecting her first child, she occasionally asked my mother for advice.

She was a tall lady with brown eyes and dark, short hair. In fact, it was very short, much shorter than the fashion of the day, but obviously it was to her liking. We became quite friendly with the young lady whom I shall call Frau Ilse, although, of course, we did not address her by her Christian name, which would have been considered an uncalled for familiarity. The young woman was intelligent and well educated, and for that very reason we found it a little difficult to believe what she told us. She simply did not seem to be the type to tell tall stories.

One day she said, 'My husband and I have been in a concentration camp, (these were prisons for political prisoners, or so we were told at the time) for a short while.'

That, of course, explained her very short hair, as the women's hair was cut when she became a prisoner. However, Frau Ilse told us that her husband and she had some important information, but decided that they would only reveal that information if any future children of theirs would ever be threatened in connection with the matter.

'If we speak up now,' she said, 'a mother of four will be in danger.'

She never told us what the important information was, nor who the mother of the four children was.

It all sounded very odd to me!

She went even further with her stories. Behind the gardens of our houses ran a row of allotments, and a pleasant man, who had built a small simple swimming pool, which he kindly allowed us to use occasionally, owned the garden directly bordering on to our back garden.

'Well,' Frau Ilse said one day, 'he might be a nice man, but he is an SS agent who keeps watch on me and other people.'

I believe my mother ignored what the woman was telling us, as she was fond of the young woman, and they were good company for each other.

I found out later that the concentration camps, which we thought were ordinary prisons for political prisoners, did exist. A small town near a village I visited frequently had one of those concentration camps in the main street. The inmates of the camp, under guard, of course, had to work in the area. Even people living only a few miles away thought it was an ordinary prison. The place is now a regional hospital, and is an institution for criminally insane.

It is difficult to believe that we didn't know what concentration camps were really like, but the majority of people did not know. It is certain that some people must have known, but for their own safety they would have been very careful to keep the knowledge to themselves.

'People living nearby must have known' I was often told.

In those days these infamous camps were not within walking distance of the nearest villages, and as nobody travelled much, and the use of cars were restricted, it was unlikely that anyone would get in the vicinity of the camps, let alone know what was happening. Should any sturdy soul have gone for a long walk, although people did have neither time nor inclination to go for long walks during the war, military guards would have turned them away before getting too near to the camps.

At the beginning of the war, and to my great relief, there was no fighting in the streets! Nobody was shot in front of our eyes, and nobody shot at us. Not at that stage anyway.

Strangely enough I remember the events of Kristallnacht. It was before the beginning of the war, in November 1938. The expression Kristallnacht was not used at the time, and I never heard it till well after the end of the war. But I do remember it was the dreadful night when shops, Synagogues and Jewish houses were damaged.

Soon afterwards all Jews had to wear a 'Judenstern', St. David star, on their clothes.

By an unfortunate coincidence my mother, my little sister and I went into town the morning after the mindless destruction of Jewish properties. Should anybody be of the opinion that the Kristallnacht caused people to cheer and applaud the senseless action, they are very much mistaken, people quickly walked past the broken shop windows in shocked silence.

My parents, who were born and grew up in Leipzig, which, amongst other things was the center of the fur trade, mainly conducted by Jews, counted many Jews among their friends. My mother was absolutely horrified by what she had seen.

On a visit to Leipzig, where her parents still lived, my mother had another terrifying experience. Coming home from town one day, she was pale and shaking, and could not speak for some time.

Eventually she told us with an unsteady voice what she had seen. 'I shan't forget it for the rest of my life,' she said. 'I saw Jewish families being herded along the streets. There were small children clinging to their mothers, dragging suitcases along. It was a heartbreaking sight.'

At the time I was too young to understand the full horror of the situation. Now, as a mother and grandmother, I cannot even imagine how these poor women suffered. Evicted from their homes, taken to an unknown destination with their small children by their side, and no idea what the future held for them.

Of course nobody knew at the time where these families were taken, and as the sight caused such an enormous uproar, it never happened again in daytime. In April 1940, 150000 Jews were sent to a ghetto in Lodz, Poland, a tiny area of 4 square kilometers.

Sadly this fate mainly affected the poorer Jews, as those who could afford it, had already left the country. Although not all of them did so. They were born in Germany, so were their parents, grandparents. They were Germans, and Germany was their country, and they saw no reason why they should leave it. I suppose by the time they realized their mistake, it was too late to leave.

Of course there was also the terrible case of shiploads of Jews who had made their way to what now is Israel, and were refused permission to land, because the Arabs objected. I am sure, or at least I hope, the authorities didn't know that they were sending these people to death camps, but they knew that forcing them to return meant they were sent to relentless persecution.

Another sea journey was made by a number of Jews who looked forward to a life of freedom in Cuba, but were turned away, as they were in any American port, and had to return to Germany where the great majority of them died.

Chapter Three

Our flat was not very suitable for us, and it must have been around 1940 when my father heard of a nice apartment on the other side of the river. He visited the place and agreed to rent it. In those days it wasn't customary for the whole family to see a new place before moving in, we certainly did not set eyes on it till we actually moved, but my father had drawn a plan of the place, and we were excited to move to such a spacious flat.

Once again we packed up all our belongings and moved, but this time only a short distance to a small village across the river.

In order to move the car to our new home, my father had to apply for permission and for an allocation of a few litres of petrol for the short trip. The car journey was quite a treat, but at the end of it the car was put back up on its wooden blocks. Sometimes I wonder what ever happened to it. I would be very upset if I had to walk away from my car and never see it again. But then during the war much more important things than cars were lost.

We moved into a spacious ground floor flat of a two family house.

At the back of the house was a small factory manufacturing steel cables, which were important items for the Armed Forces. The factory manager, Herr Meyer, had not been called up because his was a war important job. He lived with his wife and three children in the flat above us.

Behind the factory building we even had a small garden with a wonderful black cherry tree, the fruit of which were a very welcome addition to the ever-decreasing food rations.

Horst continued at the grammar school he had joined when we moved to Magdeburg, but I changed schools once again.

My journey to my new school meant walking to the station, a train ride, and another walk. Actually it was great fun, and thinking back, I feel very sorry for the adults who had to commute by train, with all us noisy pupils overrunning the small station. Although, at that stage there were few adults commuting as most of the men had all been called up.

On our outward journey we had the choice of two trains, one coming on the main line from Berlin, the other on a sideline. Needless to say, almost daily, one joker took it into his head to shout 'first train on platform 3', and everybody rushed to that platform. When the train actually arrived on the correct platform everybody was now on the wrong one. The boy who shouted in his loudest voice was the local grocer's son, who suffered from a severe stammer, which didn't bother him one little bit. As I said, it must have been a pain to the adults, but we had a marvellous time.

I quickly made friends at the new school, and was happy to attend.

Our education at that stage was very comprehensive. It covered all the scientific subjects, such as Biology, Chemistry, Mathematics, Physics, Geography and History.

We were taught German, English, and French and naturally we grumbled about having to learn English and French. What a waste of time that was, considering that we would never meet an American, Englishman or Frenchman in all our lives.

Frau Ilse, who visited us occasionally with her small daughter, overheard me grumbling one day and said, ' nonsense, you have to learn foreign languages, when you grow up you will marry an Englishman, American or Frenchman.'

The statement took my breath away. What utter rubbish. She might as well have said you will travel to the moon, and in those days such opinions almost amounted to treason.

Apart from the subjects mentioned above we were also instructed in practical matters, such as needlework, cooking, this was plain home cooking, gardening and baby -care, and of course sports activities.

The cooking was plain indeed as there were only the smallest amounts of food allocated for the cooking lessons, which was later dropped from the curriculum altogether.

Much more time was allowed for sports, which covered a comprehensive range of physical activities.

Gardening lessons were a nightmare. A friend of mine and I kept well to the back of the assembled pupils walking through the school garden. There was always the danger one would be asked to identify a certain plant, and recognizing plants was not my strongest point.

In order to get a leaving certificate one had to pass in all subjects. So it was an extensive education indeed. The drawbacks were the teachers we had.

Many of them were past retiring age, but had to stay on because the younger ones were now serving in the Armed Forces. Even the female members of staff were all elderly, and obviously not enthusiastic about having to stay on instead of enjoying retirement.

The Headmaster taught history, if one can call it that. He touched on historical subjects occasionally and then announced that girls don't have to bother about learning historical dates! I don't think anybody was keen enough to contradict him. He never bothered, or perhaps he was not able to make the subject interesting.

Despite his poor history teaching he was very keen to observe party holidays, such as Hitler's birthday and so on, although holiday is not the right word. We didn't get a day off school to stay at home. Workers went on marches and pupils attended special ceremonies at school. I'm not sure, but I think it was also on those days that money was collected, as it is now collected for charities. I imagine at that stage it was to collect money for the war effort. If you donated you got a rather attractive decorative pin, and if you were not wearing one you one got odd looks. These pins were usually beautifully carved wooden broches, which many people kept on a framed piece of velvet.

Yes, the headmaster was very keen on these activities indeed, but his teaching left a lot to be desired. His idea of history was to discuss the present, i.e. war news. Where were our troops, what had they achieved? So, I'm afraid we badly missed out on actual history lessons.

The small place where we lived was quite different from the normal German villages, which are usually occupied by farming population only. This village was divided into three parts.

First of all there was an area of beautiful detached houses mainly owned by people who conducted business in Magdeburg but preferred to live across the river. Next was the old village, we lived at the very end of this part of town. Then, divided by a large field, there was the Arbeitersiedlung, (labourers´ estate), an estate of small, simple detached houses.

I don't think people can imagine what that really means. As I mentioned before, houses were only owned by the richest of the rich. And here we had a detached house for a labourer. It was simply unheard of. And of course all labourers had a job.

There was no unemployment for anyone!

When thousands were fighting for survival after the crippling inflation, Hitler came to power, provided work for everybody, and built houses for ordinary labourers.

No wonder Hitler got support from so many ordinary people.

My father, who had fought in the first war, had lost his inheritance, had been unemployed, admired Hitler for what he had done for the people. He didn't agree with party politics, and certainly never joined the party, the SA or SS, but he did admire the man, and was bitterly disappointed at the end of the war when he learned how he had badly misjudged him.

´Never, never, will I get involved in politics again´ he would say repeatedly after the war.

On the other side of this were my grandparents and an uncle who couldn't stand Hitler, or anything he stood for, from the start. My grandmother made a strong point of forbidding any political conversation in her house in order to avoid verbal clashes, to put it mildly.

I don't know why my grandparents were against Hitler from the word go. Maybe my grandfather did not appreciate what the man had done for the people, because his business did not go under in the inflation, and my grandparents were comfortably situated. Another reason might be because my grandmother was perhaps a bit of a snob and had no time for that ´upstart´. I shall never know the truth now, but the fact remains that my grandparents were no Hitler fans, nor was my uncle.

Needless to say, my friends and I couldn't care less one-way or the other. There was no room for politics in a teenager's life, not that the word ´teenager´ was known in Germany at that stage. The German word was ´Backfisch´, meaning neither fish nor flesh, but it is obviously totally out of fashion because I can't even find it in the dictionary now. Even if the word teenager had been known in Germany, it would have been out, as all foreign words were. Expressions, which had been used for ages, had to be translated into German. That even applied to grammatical terms, and all correspondence had to be carried out in the German script.

To come back to our village, we loved living there, and had a good time. Life was much more relaxed than in the city.

Unlike my brother's Jugendweihe, my friends and I attended weekly lessons, given by the parish priest in the church hall, to be prepared for a real church confirmation. Girls attended those lessons and boys, who naturally did not concentrate very hard, were very much frowned upon by the priest.

Although the bombing of larger towns was in full swing we had not suffered many attacks at that stage. In fact, my friends and I even went to Magdeburg for 'Tanzstunde' (Dancing Lessons), which was a German tradition for young people. I attended a course of ballroom dancing lessons, which included instructions in the correct social behaviour. Before the war, the pupil's 'passed out' at a great ball, but that was not possible during the war, and we had a special evening where parents were invited to see what we had learned. When I say parents, it amounted mainly to mothers, as there were few fathers around.

We also took train rides to Magdeburg to visit cinemas, which was practically the only entertainment left. Although not quite 14, we bravely marched along hoping not to be questioned about our age. A good many films were considered to be unsuitable for people under 14.

In good weather a group of young people went swimming in a small river, and, of course, we visited our charming small local cinema. The availability of food and clothing was reducing all the time, and the rations never stretched far enough. Bread presented a special problem. My brother was very tall and could easily have managed to devour the bread ration for the whole family. To subsidize the food supply, we walked miles to the next village to buy strawberries and asparagus when in season.

We had to walk along the railway line through a small wood, and I remember clearly, that sometimes it felt quite eerie to be far away from everybody amongst all those trees. Supposing one met a dangerous looking stranger? Fortunately we never did. Not that there were that many dangerous looking strangers about in those days.

In the spring of 1942 it was my turn to be confirmed. The Sunday before the actual confirmation was the examination when we were asked questions relating to the instructions we had received the previous year. It was customary to wear a dark dress for both the examination Sunday as well as the confirmation, and it must have been very difficult for my mother to save up clothes coupons to have two dresses made. But she managed, and in my new dress I walked to church with my family two Sundays in a row.

After the ceremony we had a small family party with my parents and one of my Godmothers present, and I received small gifts. After all those years I remember clearly that my parents gave me a golden

Swiss wristwatch, and my godmother gave me a ring and a silver bracelet. As it was extremely difficult to acquire any present, the gifts were very much appreciated.

Even at that stage, shortage of food and clothing apart, the war did not bother us greatly.

There came a time when it was hinted that in future the same clothes had to be worn by everybody, in other words a kind of uniform. It would not have worked. People would have started to alter what they had bought, and would have tried to put a personal stamp on the items.

No doubt, adults got more and worried at that stage, but like all teenagers, we were more concerned with whatever occupies young people's minds.

At one end of our village was a café, and some wild rumour started that one could actually get a cup of ersatz coffee and a slice of cake, by producing a ration card. So the lady upstairs with her children, my mother, my sister and I trooped along.

We were amazed, it had not been a rumour! We really got a slice of cake. No doubt the quality was poor, but the fact of being able to sit down and being served with a cup of coffee and a slice of cake was too good to miss. We went on several of these outings till the supplies dried up.

When I reached the age of fourteen my friends and I changed from the Jungmädel to the BDM, Bund Deutscher Mädel. (Association of German girls.) We wore a dark skirt, white blouse, and a black triangular scarf rolled up and held together with a toggle, like the boy scouts. If required we wore a brown jacket. At least I think it was brown but I would not swear to that fact. Research shows me that senior leaders wore a smart dark skirt with a matching jacket and a white blouse for ordinary occasions, and a dark blue dress with matching cape and hat for festive occasions. I have never seen either. Obviously I never crossed the path of senior leaders.

I read somewhere that you only missed the BDM meetings at your peril; in fact, not attending could lead to being arrested. I am not saying it never happened, but I never heard of any particular case, nor do I know anybody who ever got into trouble for not attending. I remember a friend of mine, who lived in Magdeburg where things were stricter, got away with barely attending any of the BDM meetings. How she managed I don't know. In general one was expected to give a reason for staying away, and schoolwork was always the best excuse.

At those weekly get-togethers we had first aid lessons, listened to some talks, and talked a lot of nonsense as young girls do. Oddly enough I remember one talk very clearly which was given by a Protestant nun. The lady swore that she had looked into heaven, which had been too beautiful a sight to describe. Considering that religion was not a favored subject at the time, it is difficult to understand how the nun came to address a BDM group in the first place.

Like all young girls we usually had a good giggle at the meetings. One of the most interesting items of discussion was the fact that one of the girls, who can't have been more than 16 at the outside, was engaged to an Air force Officer. That subject beat everything else in sight.

I must stress that in spite of what one can read in many accounts, nobody trained us for any war activities, and that also went for the boys. Neither my brother nor any of our friends were ever trained in using weapons. I am not saying it never happened, but I have no personal experience of any of those activities.

Apart from the weekly meetings we had to wear uniform at school on special occasions, such as official holidays and Hitler's birthday, for instance. Wearing the uniform wasn't a problem, but singing was. Singing all the required anthems was a tiring affair, because one had to raise one's right arm in the Hitler salute, and one gradually reached the stage where one had to support the right arm with the left.

Chapter Four

The war was lasting a lot longer than everybody had expected, the time came when Horst was old enough for military service. It was definitely something my mother had hoped would never happen.

He joined the Navy as a cadet in 1942, and did his initial training in Gotenhafen, a town on the Baltic Sea, not far from Danzig.

Travel restrictions cannot have been in force at that stage, or it was easier to get a travel pass. I went to visit him in the summer holidays. It was a glorious summer, and I stayed in a youth hostel, but spent most days on the beach. I met other people visiting cadets, amongst them a very lively girl from Vienna. One day we took a day trip, again without difficulties, to pay a visit to the town of Danzig. Apart from rationing and blackouts, the war had not greatly touched that beautiful city.

During our visit we climbed to the top of a church to admire the view, and I found out that I had no head for heights, unlike the Vienna girl, who climbed up on the balustrade to take photographs. I pressed myself very hard against the back wall, and to this day remember the frightening walk down the circular staircase.

In the evenings after duty Horst came to meet me, and we shared a simple meal, went for walks, and even attended a theatre performance, which was almost unheard of in those days. Nobody worried back then about skin, and many people spent all day on the beach, acquiring a beautiful sun tans.

I remember those few weeks as a lovely holiday, the only holiday I enjoyed during the war.

Soon after I visited Horst, he had finished his initial training and was attending the Mürwik Naval School, the German equivalent of the British Naval College at Dartmouth. Horst always had the ambition to become a doctor, and hoped to study while serving in the Navy, but those in charge persuaded him to drop the medical idea and take up straightforward naval training. No doubt there was a greater need for ships officers than medical personnel.

When he passed out of the college he was posted to an active service station, and my mother began to worry seriously. She waited eagerly for his letters, it did not matter how short they were, just to tell her that he was all right.

At the end of 1942 the doctor decided that I had to have my tonsils removed, which was quite common practice in those days. My father had not been called up at that stage, and took a morning off work to accompany me to the doctor's surgery. This involved a walk to the station, a train ride and another walk before we reached our destination.

I had a light anesthetic rested a short time after the small operation in the surgery, and we started the return journey, the walk to the station, a wait for the train on the draughty platform, and then the walk home.

There was no taxi in sight anywhere!

Foreign films I have seen, depicting that time, show people happily riding around in taxis to parties and nightclubs. In my experience nobody threw parties or went out to a nightclub open during the war in Germany. Maybe the high political leaders enjoyed a more exciting social life and had the use of transport, but I know for a fact that if there were taxis, they were not for the use of the general population, not even for medical appointments.

My father returned to his office, and soon after he left I had a massive hemorrhage. Needless to say my mother was less than pleased when we went for a check-up several weeks later and the doctor thought I looked rather pale. Actually it wasn't the doctor's fault. There simply was no transport available, and it was out of the question to take up a hospital bed for a minor operation.

Soon after my operation my father was called up. He had served in a cavalry regiment in the First World War, but now he joined the administrative branch of the Navy, and was posted to Paris where he worked in an underground office, and was billeted in house not far from where Josephine Baker lived.

The mail service was not terrific, but we got the odd letter, from time to time, anyhow. As time went on, communications ceased, and while we actually thought my father stayed in Paris the whole time, we never got the message that he had been posted to Norway, a fact we didn't learn until after the end of the war.

Waiting for the mail in the morning now became the most important part of the day, and I remember clearly how relieved when there was a letter from my father or brother, or on the odd occasion, from both.

By 1943 the air raids on Berlin had increased, and as we were on a direct flight path to the German capital, we certainly spent a good deal of time in air raid shelters while the planes flew over. Fortunately not many bombs were dropped in our area at that stage. We mainly found incendiary bombs, which were small metal sticks that one picked up and threw into open spaces.

At the beginning of the air raids we used the cellar of our house as a shelter and sat in the doorways, on the theory that the extra structure would give more protection. We put pillows on our heads to protect against falling light debris. When the hated sirens screamed to announce the end of the raid we would undertake a tour of the house, checking for damage. Once my mother declared that the object lying under the table in the conservatory did not belong to her.

It turned out that it was an unexploded bomb, and mother was absolutely correct. But what was to be done with it?

It could not remain where it was, and one brave soul picked it up gingerly and carried it very carefully to the end of the property, far away from the house, and put it down. For all I know, it is still there!

By then, relations of ours, who lived in the Rhineland, were suffering continuous air raids. Eventually they were bombed out, their house was destroyed by bombs, and they were homeless. My aunt and one of her daughters came to stay with us for a short time, while my uncle and the other daughter stayed in Düsseldorf. My uncle could not desert his business, and my cousin; a chemical engineer could not leave her job at the Persil works.

While looking for more permanent accommodation they were put up by some friends. It was the first time that we provided accommodation for somebody who lost their home during air raids, but it was definitely not the last time. When my uncle had found somewhere for his family to live, my aunt and cousin went back to their home town to be with the rest of the family, even though they experienced many more bomb attacks than we did.

In spring 1943 school came to an end, and we sat our final examinations. I parted company with my friends, and it was many years later till I saw some of the girls again, in some cases more than fifty years later.

Now was the time to look towards the future. My aim was to become a dress designer, and I studied brochures from a college in Berlin. My mother was not at all happy about the idea, as Berlin suffered many air raids.

However, nothing could be decided straight away, because girls had to do a Pflichtjahr (year of duty) on leaving school. It meant one had to work for one year in a farm household, or a kinderreich family. Kinderreich means a family with many children, four at least to qualify, and kinderreich families were very popular.

Those in the powers in charge were encouraging people to have many children. I can't vouch for the truth of this story, but we heard that SS personnel who had been married, for some time, and not produced any children, had to get a divorce and find another partner to start a family. Another story reported, and again I am not sure whether it was true or not, that there were holiday camps where blond, blue-eyed men and women met, solely to create the pure Aryan race.

In our personal case we had the situation where my mother expected her fourth child, and therefore was entitled to get help, and it seemed practical that I spent that year at home, rather than going elsewhere and my mother employing a stranger. Employing might not be the right word, because I don't think pay was involved. Anyhow, the idea seemed sensible to us, but it took quite an effort to persuade the authorities to give their permission.

Not long after I left school my mother had the baby, and it was a beautiful sunny Sunday in May 1943 when my new little brother, Hasko, was born. I was fifteen at the time, and my sister, Helga, was five. As was customary in those days, my mother gave birth at home, and to get out of the way I took my sister to what would now be called a market garden where we spent all day picking gooseberries. I can't remember what we did with all those gooseberries, but I imagine we preserved them, as there was no sugar to make jam or jelly.

We must have had some sandwiches and something to drink, and no doubt we got very bored as the day went along. However, when we got back home, there was that little baby boy, and it fell to me to look after my mother, Helga and a new baby, which was quite a daunting task. In fact it was much more than my mother could have asked a strange girl to do.

The midwife came daily to take care of the medical side, but I was responsible for preparing meals and keeping the place clean, and my little sister was a great help indeed! She would watch whatever I did and then announce,

'My Mummy does it differently. '

I do not wish to give the impression that I was overburdened. I loved doing what I did, and my mother urged me not to overdo things. The most frightening task was changing the baby's nappies. I was scared stiff I might do something wrong and hurt the small thing. But nothing untoward occurred and I got used to the task. Perhaps more daunting was the fact that my grandfather came to stay for a few days, and I had to cook for him as well.

He was a connoisseur and there were few ingredients to produce a decent meal. I had little experience in cooking and it was a mammoth undertaking, but passed off well.

Now that we had a new baby we needed a pram. I announced that I was going to Magdeburg to buy one, and was told by everybody, not to waste my time.

'There is a war on and no prams to be had anywhere, ' I was told.

Undaunted and armed with the birth certificate I set off and visited every shop in Magdeburg selling prams. For a start I got a lot of dirty looks, but when I

produced the birth certificate, which made it clear that
I was not talking about my child, people were
friendlier, but had no prams to sell. I went on and on
till I came to a small shop with two or three prams on
show.

Success at last!

Again I received many suspicious looks, and one or
two awkward questions. I got the impression that they
wished the prams weren't openly on show. Only when
I persuaded them that the pram was for my brother and
not for my baby, proving the fact by producing the
birth certificate, they sold me a pram.

I was so happy I had actually managed to buy a
pram. Strictly speaking it was a glorified cardboard
box on wheels, but that's all one could expect in those
days, and I very proudly went home with my prize
purchase.

Chapter Five

By 1943 food supplies had dwindled even more. The margarine supply for a month was 120 gram, which is roughly 4 ounces, and ersatz coffee was dished out in 20gr. portions, amounting to less than an ounce. Jam coupons were split up into 25gr. portions, just below an ounce, sugar into 50 gr. which was less than two ounces. We received 25gr. pulse, and 50gr. bread coupons, but butter was measured in 5 grams, roughly a fifth of 1 ounce. There were certainly no overweight people walking about during the war.

Of course producing the ration card didn't mean we actually got what the card said we could have. My mother and I took turns in queuing at the shops for many hours. What happened if they ran out of goods by the time one reached the front of the queue? It was hard luck!

Also getting to the shops wasn't easy, it meant a fair walk, as there was no public transport. Occasionally I went on my bike, but that was not possible when I took the pram along.

Often those shopping outings were curtailed by air raid warnings. The queuing population quickly dispersed and made a mad dash for their chosen shelter, or the nearest one if necessary.

Ration cards included coupons for soap, if that was what one could call it. I shall always remember the hard grey lumps, which looked a bit like sand stuck together with glue. No doubt it vigorously massaged the skin, but it certainly did not foam.

Now that there was a baby in the family we got special supplies, which included a bar of baby soap. It was a fairly big piece, but feather light, and while it foamed like real soap it was used up in no time at all. However tempted one was, it had to be strictly reserved for the baby.

I had made some pretty covers for the pram cushions with new material bought with the special baby clothing coupons. My memory tells me it was white material with a small blue pattern.

Driven by necessity it was the time that I started learning to sew. I used old sheets and transformed them into covers for the cot. I turned dresses inside out, and cut them down for my Helga to wear. At one stage I discovered that one of my father's herringbone pattern coats revealed a tartan type pattern on the inside, and I made it into a coat for myself. We found use for everything we could lay our hands on. Underwear was a problem, it had to be repaired and repaired. But stockings were the worst. They had to be darned and darned, and eventually one embroidered a cross- stitch pattern to cover up all the darned patches.

Shoes were another serious problem. They just had to last and last, and very often we took them all to the cobbler. Our particular shoe repairer had his workshop behind Magdeburg railway station, and when the station was hit during a bomb attack, the surrounding shops, including the shoemaker's place, were destroyed as well.

Of all the bad luck the raid would have to happen when we had taken most of our shoes to be repaired.

While we didn't have a wide selection of shoes before, we were now left with the one pair we wore at the time.

To return to the subject of sewing and repairing clothes, we had a woman who came once a month to take care of all sewing requirements. The sewing machine was set up in the conservatory, and the sewing lady would treadle away merrily.

On one of her visits she told us a strange story.

It might not be generally known that not all men joined the SS voluntarily, but were called up to join those units. The sewing lady's son-in- law was one of those men.

'My daughter's husband gets thinner and thinner every day, and he looks awful, ' she said, ' and that is since he has been posted to a concentration camp. '

'Why? ' We asked.

'Well, I don't know ' she said, 'but he says that terrible things happen in the camp, and it breaks his heart to be forced to watch it, but he can't speak out, because if he did, his whole family would be in danger. '

We didn't know what to make of her story which sounded very much one of Frau Ilse's stories. At that time we thought the young man was a bit of a weakling and not cut out for military service. We thought that surely he should be glad to be in a safe position. After all he had a much easier time than the soldiers fighting at the front. But we couldn't understand why should he get thin and look ill.

The sewing lady stopped coming when there was no more material to be had for making clothes.

Chapter Six

By the winter of 1943 it seems it was a miracle that there still was some fuel for the central heating boiler. It was not particularly good fuel and there was not enough, but at least we had a certain amount of warmth. In fact when our flat had warmed up, we were asked to turn off the radiators, so some heat could find its way upstairs. But needless to say, we were glad when winter made way for spring and warmer weather.

It was in that year my sister Helga started school. German children started their education at Easter after their sixth birthday. That might sound rather late, but it was learning from the word go. No playing with toys and in the sand pit, but down to reading, writing and arithmetic from the beginning.

Like the shops, the school was a fair walk away, and as I have said there were no buses, but as there was practically no road traffic it was quite safe for the children to walk to school. Helga and the twin boys, who lived upstairs, walked to school and back together. Sadly, it wasn't long after my sister started school that those visits had to be abandoned.

On one of those walks the children saw an airplane coming straight at them. One of the boys shouted,

'Jump, jump.'

And they ran to the nearest house and crouched on the outside window sill of a cellar window frightened out of their wits, and were still very shaken and frightened when they eventually came home.

Air raids increased markedly, and it soon became too dangerous for children to go to school. While our village was not a target as such, it was unfortunately placed on the main railway line to Berlin, and near a tank supply depot. Whenever planes had some bombs left over for whatever reason, they dropped them indiscriminately, and if you were in the way that was just too bad.

My duty year was nearing its end I had to look forward to my future training, but my dream of becoming a dress designer had to be shelved. The college I had chosen was not considered war important, so the place was closed down.

Also in 1943 was the year of the Battle of the Ruhr, the bombing of Hamburg, increased attacks on Berlin, and the disastrous destruction of the Möhne and Eder Dam, highly celebrated in Britain as the Dambusters raid.

No doubt it had been an important triumph for the British war effort, but there was little reason for celebrating in Germany. I don't think people ever took time to think what effect the dam busting had on the civilian population. I only know of the terrible situation where many dead women and children were hanging in the trees. I have learned since that the attacks didn't even harm the war effort to the extent that had been expected. A British couple that visited the Möhne Sea told me recently that they could never bring themselves to watch the dam buster film again.

As I couldn't train to be a designer, I had to look elsewhere for a future career, and started training to become a chemical engineer.

The first stage of training consisted of working and studying in the laboratory of a factory, which was actually a branch of the Persil works.

The works were in a town on the main rail line to Berlin, which unfortunately was ideal at that time.

My day was divided between carrying out small tasks in the lab, and attending lectures given by one of the engineers.

While the training itself was not particularly strenuous, it involved a long day. It started with a walk to the station, followed by an hour's train journey, a walk to the factory, work in the lab, and at the end of the day the lengthy return trip. With little nourishment this routine proved to be too much for me, and I became ill, and had to take it easy for several months.

When I recovered, there was little point in looking for further training, as it would take me far away from home, which was not what I wanted. I preferred to stay close to home to help my mother with the children during the air raids.

As I had shelved any career plans for the time being, I got a job in the local railway station.

The duties were divided between general office work, operating the telegraph, and even occasionally manning the ticket counter.

In order to read and send messages on the telegraph one had to learn the Morse code, and sending information involved developing a certain knack to operate the machine. I clearly remember being told that the action had to come from the movement of the wrist. So after a short training time I hammered away at the telegraph and read the yards and yards of thin yellow paper ribbon of the incoming messages. What a pity we didn't have computers at that time. Incoming and outgoing e-mails would have been a lot easier and quicker!

The station was in the charge of the stationmaster, who was a youngish man. I wondered why he didn't serve in Armed Forces, but it was hardly a question a lowly employee could ask. I can only assume that he was not fit for military service because of health reasons, or his job was considered war important.

I'm sure that he was good at his job, but brave he was not. I recall the day when the first Stukas flew overhead. The noise was deafening, and in a flash our stationmaster dived under his desk. No doubt he thought it was a bomb. Perhaps his action wasn't so stupid after all, but the girl I worked with and I dissolved in uncontrollable giggles. The girl I just mentioned was in fact a classmate of mine who had chosen the railway as her career and happened to do her initial training at the station of our small village, but lived with her mother on the other side of the Elbe in Magdeburg.

Another member, a young woman not much older than me, was in charge of signaling of the trains.

The job was not as boring as I had imagined, and we saw several interesting trains pass through our station and one of them sticks clearly in my mind. The passengers of that particular train were a group of famous film stars of the time, and for a teenager that was an exciting sight indeed.

While quite interesting, the job was also a little scary, as it involved night work. During the night shift there was a supervisor and one other staff on duty. So on night shifts I found myself in the company of the supervisor, a girl of about twenty. Occasionally I had to take telegraph messages to the signal box in pitch darkness, which was not the most pleasant task.

As dark as it was, I was not afraid of burglars or muggers. It was all a question of survival and crime did not seem to figure largely. I'm sure such things must have happened, but I have never heard of anything being stolen from houses while the occupants were taking shelter somewhere.

At that time many people wandered from shelter to shelter, trying to find the safest place. Several used to spend the air raids in the tunnels between the station platforms on the theory that if the structure was strong enough to hold up trains, it would be protection against bombs. I personally never stayed at the station, but started to run home as soon as the sirens howled to help my mother to get the children ready for the trip to the air raid shelter.

We had given up sheltering at home, and put Helga and the twin boys from upstairs in a bicycle trailer, and little Hasko in his pushchair, to push or pull them to the 'chemical mountain'. This mountain had been formed by chemical waste, and was not solid, but springy, and considered to be completely bomb proof.

In fact it once got a direct hit without causing any damage.

On top of the mountain a company of anti-aircraft people were stationed, who operated the powerful searchlights. Apart from the Commanding Officers they were mostly girls. Needless to say when the bombs began to drop the girls came rushing down into the shelter.

I suppose, strictly speaking, it was a desertion of their duty, but they quite wisely said if anybody wished to stay on top to catch the bombs, they were welcome to do so, but it would not be one of them.

As with most things, there was another side to our safe shelter. It had been extremely difficult to dig tunnels into the mountain at low level, which had been achieved, but what could not be cured was the fact that the tunnels were invariably filled with ground water up to knee height. So we were safe, but wet and cold. My mother and I took turns in wearing my father's gumboots, which were the kind one could wear over ordinary shoes. Unfortunately there was only one pair, so while we carried the children one of us always had wet legs.

Going to the shelter was not without obstacles. We had to walk along the railway lines, cross them at one point, and walk along a lane with only a few houses, till we came to another railway line. And that is where the trouble started. Almost invariably a goods train blocked our way. It was then a question of climbing over, or crawling underneath, never knowing if the train would move or not.

The soldiers stationed at that site were our salvation. They helped us across, and I recall when I handed my baby brother to one of them under the train, he said,

'Don't worry, if the train ever starts, I will lie flat on the ground with the baby underneath. '

Thankfully that occasion never arose.

One night we stumbled out of the shelter in the dark after a bomb had hit it. I pushed the pushchair and found my way blocked by an obstruction, which made a funny noise. Guarded torchlight revealed it to be a live power line, which lay on the ground. It was purely by a lucky chance that I am still here to tell the tale.

Miraculously, the baby and the pushchair didn't come to any harm. How the pushchair survived I shall never know, considering that it was a tottery affair at the best of times. It broke down with monotonous regularity, and had to be fixed many times by the local blacksmith. But, fortunately on that fateful night it stood up to the task. Did the rubber wheel covers save us from any harm? I don't know, but am very relieved that neither the baby nor I were harmed.

Another occasion of getting to the air raids is still vividly in my mind.

We were walking along the lane towards the shelter with the trailer and pram, when we were attacked by low-flying aircraft and had to dash into the nearest of the few houses in the street.

I have been asked since what kind of plane it was, but we didn't take the trouble to inquire who they were and where they came from, nor did we stop to suggest the pilot had his eyes tested, as I would imagine it would be difficult to mistake a group of women and children for a military unit. But it was war, and unforgivable actions were not reserved for one side only.

Perhaps it is fair to say, that as a rule, American bombers attacked during the day, and British planes during the night.

As we reached the nearest house, we joined the occupants in their cellar, and it was the only time we ever came across a hysterical person.

Normally people had no time for hysterics, but got on with the job of survival. On that night, the lady of the house had other ideas. She walked up and down, up and down clapping her hands over her head and shouted,

'We'll all be killed, we'll all be killed, ' till we almost reached breaking point and thought we'd been better out in the open being shot at.

After the all clear we were extremely glad to make our way back home. Of course, on many occasions we had hardly reached home, when we had to rush back to the shelter.

As the air raids became more frequent we could not afford the time to undress, and slept fully clothed, which was quite common practice with many people. It gave the grownups a few precious moments to dress the children.

My footwear now consisted only of a pair of my father's boots. Once in a while I indulged in the luxury of taking off the boots at night, which meant losing valuable seconds.

By 1944 Magdeburg had suffered severe bomb damage, and many people lost their homes and we had a family living with us in the spare rooms. The girl I worked with was amongst them. She and her mother occupied one of our living rooms, and we all shared the kitchen. I should absolutely hate sharing my kitchen with strangers, and I'm sure my mother can't have been happy about the situation, but it had to be done.

One night the girl living with us and I had both been working late at the railway station, and when the sirens sang out we rushed home along the railway lines.

The sky was alight with what we called ´Christmas trees´. Devices dropped by the airplanes to light up the target areas.

Suddenly a man shouted, ´ Get down here, it's the only possible shelter.´

Down here, turned out to be a huge pipe underneath the railway line. It was winter, and the water in that pipe was frozen. All three of us crawled in, and slithered from one end to the other driven by the blast of the bombs.

Apart from the bombs we were not too happy to be in close contact with a complete stranger, and had no idea where he had come from, but this was not the time to ask silly questions. As it was, when things went quiet, he soon left. We on the other hand waited a long time before we dared to emerge and run home on shaky legs. Needless to say our mothers were worried sick wondering what had happened to us.

Chapter Seven

Waiting for the morning mail, as I mentioned before, was the most important time of the day for all women, who hoped daily to get a message from their men telling them that they were all right.

Unfortunately, it could also be a very sad occasion when a letter arrived announcing the death of a father, brother, husband or son.

I remember a woman living in the village, a mother of eleven children, receiving one of those letters. One of her sons had been killed in action. The poor woman was inconsolable, and hysterical with grief. It was near that time that a British plane crashed near the village and when the pilot bailed out he had to be whipped away by the police, because the bereaved mother was ready to go for him and make him personally responsible for the loss of her son.

The biggest part of the day was now spent in making our way to the air raid shelter. In our case it became more and more difficult. My mother found walking very painful, and urgently needed an operation on her foot. She point-blank refused to consider the operation, which would have meant a stay in hospital, and that was something she wouldn't consider, because she didn't want to leave me alone with my Helga and brother.

So, every time the dreaded sirens rang out, we had the same argument.

My mother would say, 'Go along with the children, and I'll stay here.'

I always replied, 'No way, we all go, or we all stay.

So mother hobbled along as best as she could. On the rare occasions when my father was on leave, his help was invaluable, but as I said, those occasions were rare indeed, and we had to get on with it as best as we could.

By 1944 things had reached a sad state. Food supplies became less and less, there was no form of entertainment whatsoever, and as far as I remember our small cinema had closed down. Not that we felt like being entertained, nor did we have the time for it. Our days were spent between queuing at the food shops and running to the shelter.

One bright spot was the fact that the people upstairs kept a pig in one of the outbuildings, and the poor beast was fed to bursting. Once in a while all gates were shut; the pig was let out for a thorough cleaning of the sty, and then came the terrible job of catching the huge animal to lock it up again. The family didn't get meat coupons, and had to hand over some of the meat when the pig was slaughtered. I can't even think where they got the food for the pig, but they obviously did. They also kept chickens, which were periodically counted by the authorities. It amounted to an act of bravery when some of them were hidden while the counting was in progress. It certainly was not an easy task, as there was always the fear that they might make a noise when this counting was in process.

And then came the time when the pig was slaughtered. The day was an unbelievable treat.

Sausages were cooked in a big boiler, and we were given some of the rich, tasteful stock.

While it was possible to hide chickens, the same could not be done with pigs. I heard of cases where small pigs were secretly kept in cellars, and illegally slaughtered during the night.

Winter was approaching once again, and the central heating boiler finally gave up. It needed replacement parts, in fact the whole thing needed replacing, but that was out of the question, and spare parts could not be obtained either.

Now it was cold in the house, desperately cold. The windows had long since been shattered, by bomb explosions and were covered by the old roll- down shutters. These shutters were operated by what once had been strong ribbons. Strong was not the word to be used any longer. The ribbons were badly frayed, and broke continuously. They had to be stitched up, which was a thankless task, because one knew they would snap again in no time whatsoever, so the job had to be done again and again.

We had no electric or gas fires, and the only source of warmth was the kitchen cooker, which in that house, was the most incredible contraption.

We had never come across anything like that before, and it took a certain skill to make it work. It was a square box with a shelf at the bottom which was filled with something that looked like coal dust, and when coaxed into life, glowed and gave up enough heat to cook things slowly, very slowly. It did not have enough power to heat the room so that one would notice, but even so it was our only source of heat.

To get the required fuel was difficult, but with ever decreasing food rations, there was little cooking to do. One really ate the most incredible things at that time. The lady upstairs used Ersatz coffee grounds to fry potatoes, if one could call it that. Some people, who managed to get castor oil, used that, with unfortunate results, and people have even been known to use something like Brylcreme.

By that stage we wore everything we could get hold of to keep warm, day and night. Naturally, the nights were the worst time. As we know it is the habit of small children to kick off their covers. And that is exactly what Hasko did after we had wrapped him up in every blanket we could find. We had no choice but to get up and cover him again to stop him from freezing to death.

When I went to work in the morning, there were more and more very sad sights. Morning after morning the platforms were crowded with the first of the refugees from the East. They had walked most of the way, and were now waiting for trains to take them somewhere.

Where exactly nobody knew.

All they owned were the clothes they wore, and perhaps a small case, but many did not even have that. Unless they had friends or relations somewhere in the West, they ended up in refugee camps.

Those camps were soul-destroying places. Many people were crammed together in large rooms; often families were only separated from each other by a blanket. And many stayed there for a long, long time. A large number of refugees remained in those camps until rebuilding had started, which, naturally was not till after the end of the war. Friends of ours had spent time in one of those camps with their three children, and the mother admitted she had nearly reached breaking point until they finally found decent accommodation.

Sadly this atmosphere also affected people working in those camps. I once met a young woman who started to work in one camp full of good intentions and raring to go helping people wherever she could. After a year she was a changed person, disillusioned and hardly able to cope with the task.

Many of the refugees came from far outlying parts of Germany and didn't even speak German, which made working with them difficult. But the real trouble lay in a different direction.

After the end of the war, anybody between 18 and 80 could get a job. The country was rebuilt and there was plenty to do. But as human nature will have it, not everybody believes in work, and tries to take the easy way out.

So several gangs were formed in the refugee camps bent on committing crime, making life for those in charge of the camps very difficult.

I didn't find out till much later, that British prisoners of war, like the refugees, had walked from East Prussia till they met the British troops in the West of Germany who flew them back home. The prisoners in East Prussia were released by their German guards and told to get to the West before the Russian Troops arrived. As I said, it was not till much later till I found out about this from my husband who had been one of those prisoners. He had actually worked on a large country estate owned by a German aristocrat whose daughter was married to a German officer. When the prisoners started their walk to the West, they helped the officer's wife and children, who also tried to get away before the Russians arrived.

One morning, I arrived at work, and found a man stripped to the waist, having a wash in a bowl of water in the back office of the station. It turned out that he was a high railway official who took the opportunity to freshen up in the station. No doubt all the people who cluttered up the platforms would have been happy to do the same, but we could not accommodate them all.

It was from the first refugees that we heard about unspeakable atrocities carried out by the advancing Russian troops. It may be that they had been fighting for a long time which might account for their behaviour, and maybe for some of them it was not so outrageous, but it was a different matter for their victims.

There were many tales we heard from the refugees. A woman who didn't have time to get the baby girl from the garden as the soldiers approached. The mother hid in the firm knowledge that a baby was safe. Unfortunately she was wrong. The baby girl was raped, and killed. There was a terrible case, and I find it extremely difficult to put into words, when we were told that some soldiers nailed children's tongues to the table.

A friend of mine told me of her own experience. Her father was the manager of a large country estate in East Prussia, and they didn't get the chance to leave before Russian troops reached their area. When the soldiers entered their house, her parents shielded her by standing in front of her, but as the soldiers systematically battered her parents down. She could not stand it any longer and crawled out. She was brutally raped by four soldiers. My friend was only fourteen years old at the time, and has never been able to form a meaningful relationship since.

Another friend of mine related her experience to me after she had managed to return home safely. She had chosen to become a teacher, and attended a teacher training college in the far east of Germany. Her father, a civil servant, worked in the same area at the time. When the Russians marched forward, he rang the college and urged them to send the students home, but was told they had to wait for the official notification. He repeatedly rang back and in the end shouted,

'Official notification or not, send them home before it is too late. '

Eventually those in charge of the college gave in, and the girls struggled to the station carrying their cases, which they dropped by the wayside long before they reached the station, but it was too late, the last train had left.

The only train remaining was reserved for railway personnel. My friend ignored this and she and another girl boarded the train pretending to be railway employees, and then made their way from one end of the train to the other, hiding wherever they could, in desperate fear of being found out. When she recounted the journey we shed tears of laughter, but it was not funny at all. However, fortunately they did manage to get to safety, and one shudders to think what happened to the girls who were left behind.

The stories are many and there is one concerning a friend of Helga. The girl's mother seemed to be in a permanent, deep depression and eventually found out that the reason is this. They were travelling on a crowded refugee train from the East, the mother, daughter and baby brother. When anybody died during the journey, they were thrown off the train. That sounds extremely cruel, but what else could they do? They didn't have a chance to bury their dead. It was totally out of the question that the train could be stopped, and nobody knew how long they would be on the train. Space was needed, and they simply could not keep the dead bodies on the train for whoever knew how long.

When the baby brother of my sister's friend died, he was taken from his mother and thrown off the train. No wonder the poor woman was depressed. It is hard to believe that a mother can ever come to terms with such a disastrous event.

To our great relief the desperately cold winter finally gave way to milder weather. Yet the relief was mingled with the concern of the Russian troops coming uncomfortably near.

Chapter Eight

With the Russian Army coming uncomfortably close, it seemed a good idea to hide some of our valuables. Fortunately my mother's bottom drawer items had survived the inflation.

One of the cellar rooms had an opening leading to a small recess, which, in better times, had been used to store wine. Now it was a perfect hiding place.

We went through the flat, and decided to start packing my mother's crockery, which was not a mean task. In my mother's day one didn't talk about four or six place settings, but only counted in dozens. To this day I remember the delicate white porcelain with a green vine leaf pattern. We packed endless items, ranging from large serving dishes to small mocha cups. I am not sure, but think we took newspapers and rags to wrap the items, as there was no way whatsoever to get any wrapping material, quite apart from the fact things such as bubble wrap were a thing of the future.

It took a fair time to pack the china, which filled a large box. Next it took our combined effort to manoeuver the heavy box carefully down the cellar steps.

After the china we concentrated on the heavy silver. I doubt silver plate was even heard of in my mother's young days. Like the green wine leaves on the china, I remember the silver pattern as well. Small silver pearls framed the handles of knives, spoons and forks. Both similar china and silver patterns have been repeated in recent years.

The silver box was not as large as the china, but it was heavy and not easy to carry into the cellar either.

Some linen followed china and silver. Bed linen, towels, tea towels and so on, also came in dozens, and some of the items originating from my mother's Aussteuer, meaning 'bottom drawer' were still unused and had been earmarked for me and Helga's bottom drawer, for when we married..

All these items were followed by two travel bags given to us into safe keeping by relations who lived in big cities, while we lived in a small village. The misguided idea was that we would experience less destruction than those living in the big towns, which was certainly the case in the early war years, but as time marched along, we were not much safer than the city dwellers, particularly as we were on a direct route to Berlin.

My uncle, who manufactured dental fillings, included two silver bars in his bag. I always wondered if those who found them recognized their value, as they really looked just like two dirty lumps of metal.

Among other things, my grandparent's bag included some jewellery, my grandfather's best watch, and some of his best shirts he was particularly fond of.

As a last thought I added our copper samovar, an impressive piece which my parents had been given by some White Russian friends. I loved the beautiful piece, and polished it often.

Thinking back, I suppose we should have carried the oil paintings, my father inherited from his parents, down in the cellar as well. Somehow the thought never occurred to us. Nor did we waste a moment's notice on

Hitler's picture, and left it where it was. If my memory serves me right, it hung between the two windows of one of the living rooms.

It was law to have Hitler's picture in the house, so we did. Why? I was asked once thinking it was a silly law.

When everybody living in the house had stored his or her goods in the small recess, we bricked it up, and rubbed dirt on the wall to make it look well worn.

Now some of our treasures were safe! Or so we thought.

At that time we were not to know that we would never see any of the beautiful things again. Nor have we ever been able to find out who discovered the recess and opened it up.

Had the Meyer family opened up before they went to the West? Had the Russian soldiers found the recess, or the people who moved into the house after the soldiers left?

From what we learnt later a whole succession of people moved in and out of the house until it was taken over by an architect who restored it, which it desperately needed.

Horst managed a visit to the house after the war and took photographs, which were a heartbreaking sight. The place was completely neglected, and looked dark and dismal, and there was no sign of the beautiful lilac trees running along the front of the house.

At some stage we heard about the fate of the lilac trees. When in bloom the trees were a magnificent sight, not to mention the fabulous scent. However, it seems the Russian soldiers did not appreciate the beauty and chopped the trees down.

As the Russian Army approached people were advised to leave. Leave, but where could they go? Many considered the possibility, but gave up because they simply couldn't bring themselves to leave everything they owned and go to some unknown destination.

We thought a short break would be a good idea, especially as my mother's foot complaint got worse, and my sister was ill as well. With that in mind my mother wrote to an aunt of hers who lived in a small town at the foot of the Harz Mountains, asking if we could come for a short rest. The aunt wrote back saying that we could stay with them for a short while.

Before we left I paid a visit to our dentist as one my teeth needed a filling.

In those days one got a temporary filling which had to be replaced by a permanent one after three days. Sadly, the dentists house got a direct hit during those three days, the dentist was killed, and it was about three months before I got the chance to see another dentist. By then the tooth was beyond repair, and the damage had spread to other teeth. Much as I hated the idea, and tried very hard to keep my teeth, the damage was too far advanced, and I lost all my teeth very early.

Shortly before we left we were met with another surprise. One morning a deep trench had been dug across every road leading out of the place. Things were really getting serious. The trenches were supposed to slow down or even stop the advancing enemy troops.

We applied for travel permission, packed the pram with necessary items for the child, and a few of our things, locked up the house, and set off, intending to return to our home soon.

Our neighbours didn't believe that we would reach our destination, and expected us back within a day or two, and that is what they told my father, who happened to be on a courier journey, and managed to call in at home. Believing we would be back soon, he carefully left all his valuable items at home, and continued his journey. However, being told where we headed for turned out to be extremely important information for him at a later date.

In spite of what everybody thought we reached our destination after an appalling journey. We travelled in overcrowded trains, mainly occupied by refugees from the East. I clearly recall a young lady dressed in riding breeches who told us that she had come from a country estate in East Prussia, and hadn't even found time to pack a small bag, but had only managed to let lose all the animals before getting away.

We'd changed trains often, hung around draughty platforms with little food or comfort, were cold and miserable, but eventually arrived at the station of the small town we'd been heading for. We learned to our cost that my great aunt's house was a fair way from the station, up on a hill. Not the most pleasant walk after a long, tiring journey, but we made it.

Chapter Nine

The small town in the Harz Mountains had not been greatly touched by the war, as there was no valuable target anywhere near. Actually, the inhabitants were greatly disturbed when a stray bomb had hit one house.

Before we left the destruction of Dresden had taken place, although we did not hear about that till much later. As far as I know it has never been established how many people were killed that night because the city was crowded with refugees.

Of course the food shortage was as bad in this small place as anywhere else, but my great-aunt and uncle did not do too badly. They had a large fruit garden, kept chickens, geese, and vicious beasts they were too. They had a milk sheep and made their own butter. I don't know what sheep butter tastes like, because their hospitality didn't stretch to sharing such delicacies with us.

We were invited to take our meals with them in the dining room, where we ate our miserable bits while they dined on food we did not even know still existed.

Needless to say after the first meal we did not join them in the dining room again. Naturally my little brother and sister wanted the nice food, which was on the table, so did my mother and I, but how to explain to the children that they could not have it? We took our meager meals in the room allocated to us, where we slept on the floor. I am sorry to say, that I thought my great aunt was the nearest thing to a witch I have ever come across, and that is in behaviour as well as looks, and her husband was not much better. He saw us as the ideal workhorses. Help in the garden; pull his handcart up and down the long steep hill for whatever reason. It was not much of a break after all, but we did sleep through the nights without having to run to the shelter, and that was something we hadn't known for a long time, but we were looking forward to going home again.

There was a company of German soldiers which occupied a large country estate house nearby. This caused mixed feelings in the town. On the one hand it meant protection, on the other they were a target, and might bring the fighting right to our doorstep.

Then one day we saw the troops move out. Now what? Were they going to confront the American troops, or were they retreating?

We were not left in doubt for long. We had instructions to go down into the cellar if we heard gunfire. And sure enough we soon did. We were told to keep the house door open. However, my great-aunt was not one to take any notice of such instructions, and had locked the door.

At the time a young woman, "a fallen woman", according to my great- aunt, who had a child without being married, lived in the house with her little girl, working as my great-aunt's maid. The young woman had been in the army, and knew it was not a good idea to ignore the instructions, and she had the good sense to run upstairs and unlock the door. It was not long before we heard heavy army boots moving about upstairs.

We were frightened that the fighting was now right on top of us. The noise came nearer, the cellar door was opened, and we heard heavy boots coming down the steps.

We stared from the darkness. They were not German soldiers, but Americans brandishing machine guns.

We had been in dangerous situations before, but I don't think we'd ever been so terrified in all our lives. As it turned out, all they wanted was to find something to drink. The sight of my great-aunt shouting 'Most, Most, we only have Most, ' meaning must or fruit juice, was too much for the American soldiers, who burst out laughing and withdrew.

We waited a good long while, and then crept up the stairs with shaking legs. For our family the war was over.

Hitler's hundred-year empire had collapsed, and the man at the helm of that empire was dead.

I'm not quite sure whether he really was at the helm. I find it difficult to believe, that any one man, particularly somebody who had not been trained to lead a country, could execute so much power. I thought that he might have been a figure head directed by a number of people. But I am told he really was an extraordinary powerful person, who was fanatical about his ideas.

Hitler joined the Deutsche Arbeiter Partei (German Workers' Party) in 1919, which became the Nationalsozialistische Deutsche Arbeiter Partei (National Socialistic German Workers' Party) in 1920 with Hitler as their propaganda leader, and in 1921 he became their leader. In 1920 the party had 64 members, who had risen to 55000 in 1923, and in 1934 Hitler was president and chancellor. So one can only imagine that he had a lot of drive from the word go.

It is supposition, but one can only imagine the reasons for his hatred of the Jews. Perhaps it stemmed from the fact that his mother was ill, had been badly treated by a Jewish doctor, and died a painful death.

There is no doubt that the Jews were not welcome in many places around the world, but nobody went to extremes that Hitler did. There were the events in Russia as far back as 1903 when the Jews were persecuted, people injured and killed. I have read that even in those times the police did nothing and society ladies drove past in their carriages to enjoy the spectacle.

Did Hitler want the Jews out of the way because he hated them so much, or simply to make way for the all-Aryan race he wanted to create? Strange for a man who hardly had any Aryan looks. It has been said that he didn't intend for all the Jews to die, but things went out of hand.

For a man who seemed genuinely fond of children, which usually does not mean he was an evil person, I wonder if he saw little Jewish children, or saw what happened to them? I doubt he visited one of the death camps or ever watched the suffering he inflicted on people?

Only a short while ago I read a letter in a newspaper when the reader was outraged by the fact that Hitler forbade fox hunting. How could the man do what he did to people and worry about animals, the reader asked. Only those close to him will know what the man was really like, and there is nobody left who was close to him, and some questions will never be answered.

One of those close to him was Eva Braun, of whose existence the German population knew absolutely nothing. If she was ever seen at his house in Berchtesgaden, one assumed that she was a secretary. The official announcement that Adolf Hitler had married a lady called Eva Braun was not made until a few days before they committed suicide.

Rumours had it that Hitler and his wife did not commit suicide, but managed to leave the country. If they did, nobody ever produced any proof that they had been seen.

We also learned that Goebbels and his whole family died, or rather, he killed his wife and children, and then committed suicide. No doubt he thought it was the best way to go, but it seems sad to think those children never got a chance to live. Goering's wife and daughter did not take that way out, but lived quietly in the south of Germany.

The news reported many things, and rumours were flying around, and there was a lot to be taken in, but mainly people were concerned with their personal affairs.

Chapter Ten

Our personal affairs were bleak. The war was over, but the hard times were not. The news on the radio reported that the Russian Troops had advanced right up to the river Elbe, meaning our home was now in the Russian sector, and we could not return. It meant that the few things we had packed in the pram for our short rest were all we owned. My parents had lost everything the second time in their lives.

Being young that did not properly register with me at the time, but I can only now appreciate how awful that must have been for my mother.

To think I would walk out of my house with a small suitcase and never come back, the suitcase being the only think I owned is too difficult to imagine. But that is exactly what had happened. We had locked the doors of our house, started our journey, hoping to come back in a few weeks, and now it was all gone.

Would we have left if we had known that would be the case? Would it have been better to hang on to our possessions and get caught up in the fighting like the people who lived upstairs, who lost one of the twin boys?

The poor boy was crossing the road when he got hit by artillery fire and his mother watched him die. Would it have been better to hang on to our goods and suffer the fate of the many women who were raped by Russian soldiers?

I will never know the answer.

Now it was a case of survival more than ever. We walked for miles to the nearest village to exchange a few pieces of jewelry for a loaf of bread, a bag of flour, potatoes and even a little fat. Of course we only had very little jewelry, as we carefully stored most of our valuables at home. When the few items were gone one could almost call those trips to the surrounding villages as begging, and it must have been one of the hardest things for my mother, who was a proud woman, to do.

When Hasko and Helga said, 'We are so hungry.' she buried her pride and carried on. Apart from anything else, it must have been extremely painful as there had been no chance to have her foot treated.

Our main meal of the day consisted of a large pot of barley flavoured with a stock cube. I have never managed to eat barley ever since.

One day it was announced that sacks of sugar were being given away at the railway station. My great-uncle hummed and hawed, saying that it could not be legal, and was not to be considered. Which I thought it was fine for him to say, as he hadn't been plagued by hunger. We took a handcart and made our way to the station. As it happened, he had been right.

It turned out that somebody had broken open a goods wagon, and people had helped themselves to the sugar. Having been law- abiding citizens all our lives, we felt very guilty, but the temptation to get sugar was too great, and we loaded a sack onto the handcart and dragged it along the long steep path up to the house. Now we had an addition to our menu. We boiled potatoes, mixed them with sugar, squashed them into a baking tin and baked them.

It made a delicious cake!

Nothing went to waste, the coarse yarn the sacks were unraveled to make knitted pullovers. I think they must have been the original hair shirts. I have never felt anything so scratchy before or since.

Fighting in the area had ceased. It was an enormous relief that nobody was being killed or injured anymore, but unfortunately it came too late for many, particularly some young boys.

One had heard a lot about young boys being called up to fight. I am not sure that it actually was the case; at least we have never come across any boy who was called up.

However, being enthusiastic, and obviously nobody had been in a position to stop them, young boys did join in the fighting towards the end of the war in the area where we now lived.

The saddest place I visited in my life is what is called the Soldatenfriedhof. ′ (Soldier's cemetery.) It is a small cemetery in a beautiful spot in the Harz Mountains.

On one occasion we visited that cemetery, and it might sound silly, but one got an eerie feeling in that totally quiet, beautiful spot. It was tragic to see that the ages of those buried were all in the early teens, and I mean early, from twelve upwards. Their life had ended before it had properly begun. What for? It had achieved nothing, simply caused pain and grief.

Fighting in the area had ceased. The American troops often passed through the place, staying a few days until others replaced them.

As we lived up on a hill, going down to the town this involved passing through what had been the administrative buildings of a former mine, and was now a Polish camp. We then followed a path with a deep drop down to a disused railway line. Along that path ran a number of stone boulders, invariably occupied by American soldiers.

Goebbel´s propaganda had been very efficient, and we were scared stiff when encountering these soldiers. As it was, they were quite harmless. They left you in no doubt as to what they wanted, but to give them their due, they took no for an answer.

We did hear about cases of rape, but I don't think it happened where we were living, or if it did, it was kept very quiet. Perhaps, as nature will have it, it wasn't necessary, because there were enough ´professional ladies´ to oblige. Many of these women were evacuees from the Rheinland. At that time I was too naive to realise what these ladies were there for.

In their defense I must mention, that being starved of anything, the temptation of getting food, cigarettes and even clothing was probably too much for anyone to refuse.

After passing the American soldiers sitting on the boulders, we went down some zigzag steps towards a wooden bridge spanning a small river. The bridge had many planks missing, and it involved balancing on the beams, which originally held the planks.

After negotiating that obstacle, we went along a path between two fields, which were extremely dusty in dry weather, and ankle deep in mud in wet weather. There simply was no way to get to town with clean shoes, and on occasion we had to go down to town several times a day.

With the bridge in a poor state of repair, it was almost impossible for one person to cross it with the pushchair. It needed two people to balance on the beams carrying the pushchair. At times the path between the fields was knee-deep in water, and we had to go a very long way round to get to town.

Apart from the material worries, we suffered desperate anxiety about my father and brother's whereabouts. We had lost all communication with them, and of course they had no way of knowing where we were.

As we were now permanent visitors, we moved into two rooms on the first floor, which really was an attic. The larger of the two was the living room, bedroom and kitchen. It had a metal stove, which could be fired with coal, but of course, there was no coal. We went into the woods and cut down small trees, which was considered a severe crime in Germany. However, under the circumstances the Forestry officials closed their eyes, simply told us, not to drag the trees, but carry them, so it couldn't be detected where they ended up.

We chopped the trees as best as we could, and used them for fuel to cook our meagre meals on top of the stove. As the trees were wet, they did not provide particularly good fuel, and we stacked the wood behind the stove in a desperate attempt to dry it out.

Mother was worried about her parents, and set out to travel to Leipzig in any way she could. At that time

Leipzig was in the Western Zone, but during her stay in Leipzig the boundaries were adjusted, and the Russian troops took over large areas, which had previously been in Western hands.

At the time we didn't know why the boundary adjustment occurred, but I have since learned the reason, was as follows. In 1943 the three Powers of Britain, USA and Russia met in Tehran and decided which part of Germany they would occupy. In the last days of fighting American and British troops advanced further than the agreement stated, and the Russians moved forward to claim their portion. Any suggestion to allocate an area to the French was strongly turned down by the Russians who told the Western Allies that if they wanted the French to have an area they would have to give up some of their Zones, and that is what happened.

After the border adjustments Leipzig was now in the Eastern Zone.

Left behind with two small children, it was an extremely anxious time for me, particularly as my Great Uncle gleefully told me my mother wouldn't come back. I don't know why it gave him so much pleasure unless he thought he now had a free hand in making us work for him.

However, I was absolutely sure that my mother would find a way to return. As it happened, she got out of Leipzig at the last minute. When her train pulled out of station, the first Russian train pulled in.

My mother's transport did not go very far, and the passengers completed their journey by walking for miles, with guides to show them the way across the border.

After a very strenuous journey my mother managed to return to us.

A sad case was in the newspapers at that time. One of the guides leading people across the border killed an enormous number of women while showing them the way across. Either he was completely evil, or severely disturbed. The fact is, reports stated that he had never seen that it was wrong what he had done.

Amongst many, the Duchess of Brunswick was also affected by the boundary changes, but I understand she was taken to the West by British troops, and lived in a house in the Hanover area. In years to come she was always a guest of honour at the annual reception given by the British Consulate in Hanover, a glamorous affair I was able to attend and enjoyed very much.

Apparently she was asked one day how she liked living in her present house, and replied. 'How would you like living in a house when you have been brought up in an emperor's castle? '

There is no answer to that.

Chapter Eleven

By some miracle we received a postcard from my
father with an address in the North of Germany.
We discussed the matter, and decided I would set out
to find him. I got travel permission, and started my
journey, a mixture of getting lifts and travelling by
train. As there was very little traffic on the roads,
getting a lift did not happen often.

Eventually I reached the address given on the
postcard.

The address was of a bridge with a large notice saying
that there were no prisoners in the area, and that it was
merely a postal address. Like other women who
looked for husbands, fathers, sons, I took no notice of
the warning, but thought it best to see for myself.

Strictly speaking I required a pass to cross the
bridge, but the British soldiers on duty were quite
happy to see any bit of paper. I produced my travel
pass, and walked along. We were now in a very large
prison camp. In fact it was not a camp at all, the whole
area held prisoners of war. German officers
commanded the various huts, and when I eventually
found my father, he was in a hut run on the lines of a
German Officers´ Mess. Having found him was the
best thing that could have happened, because I could
confirm that we now lived in the West.

Anybody who could produce an address in the West
would be released in time. Those prisoners, who could
only produce an address in the East, were shipped to
Canada.

For once fate was on our side. While we imagined my father to be in France, he had actually been posted to Norway, and he did a lot of courier service. As mentioned before, the day after we left home he was on one of his courier journeys and managed to call at the house. He was told where we were heading for, but nobody believed we would make it, and would come back home very soon.

Unfortunately expecting us to be back home shortly, he put his valuable items in his desk, which then with the rest of our goods fell into the hands of Russian soldiers.

After time he learned where we were headed, and on the off chance sent a card to that address, where it actually found us. Eventually he was released.

I stayed two days in the 'prison camp' sharing the room of a girl who'd served in the Army, and was now a prisoner of war. After the two days I started my return journey, which again, but this was not without difficulties. I got as far as Hamburg Harburg station, hoping to pick up a train going in my direction. And sure enough it was announced that a train was leaving for Braunschweig. Masses of people rushed to the platform mentioned. It was a rare opportunity not to be missed. I didn't dare visiting the washroom in case I missed it.

The train turned out to be an open goods train. That was fine. It was a lovely day, and everybody sat on the floor enjoying the sunshine. We travelled for hours and hours without stopping, which was also all right, except- there were no toilet facilities. So, when the train stopped, people didn't care whether it went off without them, but there was a mad scramble to the nearest ditch for obvious reasons. As it was, everybody boarded again before the train moved.

In the early days the American troops stayed a few days in our town before moving on, and were eventually replaced by British troops and when an English Regiment settled in quite a friendly atmosphere developed. The main street was totally requisitioned and used as quarters for the soldiers and the local inn became the Sergeants´ mess. It is natural that the people whose houses had been requisitioned were extremely upset, but other than this there was a friendly feeling between soldiers and residents.

The house next to us was requisitioned as an Officers´ Mess, which left three houses on our hill heavily overcrowded with refugees, and there were very many children.

It wasn't long for the children to make friends with the staff of the Officers' Mess. They also fed the chickens, which were kept at the foot of the garden. Surprised how long it took the children to carry out that task, the kitchen staff followed them one day. They were horrified at what they saw.

Amongst the food were crusts cut off from sandwiches. White bread with butter! It was something the children had never seen before, and they were eating all the crusts before they fed the chickens. After it had been discovered, they were strictly forbidden to ever eat the crusts again, but they all got a sandwich for feeding the chickens.

Food supplies were getting a little easier, and my mother came home one day proudly presenting some peanuts for the smaller children. So pleased to have found a special treat, she was disappointed by their reaction. They were not impressed with the peanuts.

It had never occurred to any of us that they had never seen the nuts and didn't know that they had to be peeled. They munched them with the shells on.

After the Russian Army had moved forwards my grandparents were now in the Russian Zone, and visiting them involved quite adventurous manoeuvers. It might sound quite ridiculous today, but we did not see it as an adventure, and definitely did not think it was funny.

After the adjustment of the Zones we found ourselves only a few miles away from the Russian border, which ran between two villages. Many families, who had members in either village, were now separated.

British soldiers were not allowed to get nearer than five kilometers from the Russian boarder. To reach the British Forces Leave Centre in Bad Harzburg, that restriction didn't apply to a short stretch of railway line, as it ran exactly along the Russian border.

When we wanted to cross the border we set out in the evening and walked to the village on our side. Waiting for the dark of the night we walked towards the boarder along a field at the edge of a small copse, hiding amongst the trees when necessary. It became necessary to keep hidden when we saw cigarettes glowing, belonging to Russian soldiers who were marching up and down along the border.

When we saw the glow of their cigarettes, we stopped walking, whispering, even breathing, till they moved away from us. We continued to creep along to the village on the Russian side. From there, still under cover of darkness, we walked to the nearest railway station to catch a train, hopefully going in the direction of the British Zone.

The Russian soldiers occasionally caught people on their way to the station, but usually nothing happened, and they were allowed to go. Of course they always swore that they had not crossed the border, had simply come from the next village to visit somebody. It was quite true; they had come from the next village, no need to admit that it was on the wrong side.

When my grandmother sadly died, we were determined for our grandfather to live with us. The journey involved the same procedure and the only way to get him across was the way described above. It was a hair-raising trip. He had always lived in a big town, was confused with grief, and did not understand why there was no decent transport. It is quite remarkable that the old gentleman managed the long walk and the dangerous crossing involved. He got very fed up with people creeping along in the dark on a muddy surface, and could not understand why nobody spoke up, but whispered, and only that when absolutely necessary. Eventually grandfather was safe with his family.

Many people used the crossing regularly, until the Russians dug deep trenches all along the border and put up barbed wire fences. That was the end of the night journeys across the border.

The time came when my father returned home. He put his hand to everything he could think of to support his family. He used his artistic talent to paint portraits from photographs, helped local shopkeepers with window dressing until he got another civil service job.

To our great delight my parents found a way to discover Horst's whereabouts and managed to convey our new address to him. He was actually a prisoner of war in Egypt, and being young and single, he returned very late. He joined us in our extremely poor accommodation, but soon left for university.

The big recovery started.

People worked, worked and worked to rebuild the country. Many people literary built their own houses, and there was work for everybody.

Food supplies were still very poor. In 1947 they amounted to between less than 900 to1050 calories per day. After the harvest people combed the fields for a few grains of wheat or rye, they collected beechnuts, which could be exchanged for oil.

In 1948 there was currency reform. Everybody got 40 Deutsch Marks. As the German Mark had been devalued, even if people had access to their savings, they only got 10% of the original sum. Many had lost confidence in the value of saving, and for many years did not trust banks to look after their money.

It had been almost impossible for a long time to buy any clothes, yet miraculously, when the new money was issued, shopkeepers managed to find a few articles of clothing, and that was the beginning of their future wealth.

Starved of anything new, many could not resist the temptation and used the small sum of money they had to buy the clothing on show in the shops.

Care parcels of subsidized food rations were sent to us from other countries. There was the time when everything we were sent was yellow. This was due to an interpretation error, when asked what was needed, the German authorities said, 'Korn', which is a collective expression for grain. However the American authorities took it to be corn, maize like as corn on the cob and that it what we got. Yellow flour, which made yellow bread, we cooked milk pudding with yellow semolina, and thought we were in danger of becoming yellow ourselves.

Chapter Twelve

The time came for me to think of my career plans again. My original idea of becoming a dress designer had to be forgotten. There was no way I could do the training.

It was at that stage that I saw an announcement of something called ´Aktion Nordsee´, (Action North Sea). It was a scheme allowing girls to go to England for two years.

To actually go to a foreign country and learn the language in another country was an opportunity too good to miss. I applied and stringent examinations followed. There were numerous interviews, and a clean bill of health was essential as well as proof that there was no police record.

One had three choices of jobs.

One could train to be a nurse.

Work as a ward maid.

Do domestic work.

As I had learned quite a bit of English at school, I was persuaded to take up nursing. However, in my opinion nursing is a vocation, which I do not possess. Ward maid is very near nursing, so I turned that down as well, and ended in the remote Country house of a rich Family.

The idea was that one could attend evening classes and gain a language certificate, but unfortunately we were too far away from where the evening classes were held.

However, on my time off, one afternoon a week, and every second Sunday, my friends and I (there were several German girls in the area) walked about four miles to the small town nearby, treated ourselves to afternoon tea in a small cafe, and then went to see a film. We enjoyed the action and hearing the actors speak, helped us tremendously to perfect our English language. Listening to the wireless also helped.

I spent a fair amount of time in the company of the cook, which came in handy. The cook was a woman who knew her place, which didn't stop her from stuffing anything she possibly could take from the larder in a big bag and taking it to her daughter. But she was very keen to observe the difference between upstairs and downstairs.

The lady of the house went on extensive journeys every winter, while her husband, who was too much of an invalid to travel, stayed at home. To keep him company at those times, 'Mademoiselle' came over from France. I was given to understand by the housekeeper that the owner of the house and Mademoiselle had been on very intimate terms in their young days.

One day I asked the cook ´what does Mademoiselle do?´

The cook considered it to be a shocking, question. She drew herself up to her full height and said, ´Mademoiselle does not do anything, she is a lady! ´

The two years had certainly been an interesting experience, and when I returned to Germany, I attended an interpreter college, where I gained an interpreter certificate, and soon afterwards started a job as an interpreter for the British Liaison Office in a town not too far away from where we lived.

There were a few weeks between finishing the college and starting the job, and I took that time to get a driving licence. Including the test it took twelve lessons, plus theoretical instructions on the driving instructors premises in a room specially made for those lessons. At that time decent cars were back on the road.

I remember the day, but I can't put an exact date to it, when the daughter of one of the refugees living in the house next to us on the hill, arrived with a BMW Bubble Car. I couldn't believe it, that girl had a car, a real car, and it was new, a new car! We were all speechless with admiration. I doubt one would call the Bubble Car a real car nowadays, but at the time it seemed to be a magnificent thing.

When I started my job I lived in a bed-sit during the week, but went home at weekends, driving my first car, a DKW. The gear leaver of that car looked like a pistol grip which one turned left or right. In fact it was called a pistol gear leaver.

With their usual persistence my parents eventually secured a flat down in the town, my father had a decent job, and things slowly got better, and more comfortable.

I graduated from a bed-sit to a small flat, bought a better car, and enjoyed a decent salary. Everything was definitely looking up.

Compared to now, life was very simple. We did not have televisions, washing machines, dishwashers, and other items we now take for granted. It should be said that some televisions were about, but very few, and for special occasions people used to hire a set for a day. Very few people had a telephone, and there were comparatively few cars on the roads.

The office where I worked was situated in a building called 'Behördenhaus' meaning 'authorities building'. Now requisitioned by the British Army it housed many small units, such as pay office, post office, and so on, and it was in that building that I met my future husband, George Mackenzie

George, a Major in the British Army, worked a few floors up from where my office was situated. Most days my colleagues and I would cross the road to buy our lunch from a small shop.

I didn't know at the time, but I was being watched and admired from a window. George soon started visiting the shop at the same time I was buying my lunch. We passed the time of day and soon we began to know each other better.

There were many experiences we had in common. George told me he had served in Egypt, and I told him my brother was a prisoner of war there. He then said he also had been a prisoner in Eastern Germany and when the Russians were approaching his guards helped him and his fellow prisoners to escape to the West, to join the advancing British forces.

The evening of a Staff Party came, it was a rather boring affair, and George and I started really talking, found that we liked each other's company, and both wanted to see each other again.

Love blossomed.

The words of Frau Ilse spoken many years ago came back to me.

'When you grow up you will marry Englishmen and Frenchmen. '

I didn't marry an Englishman, I didn't marry a Frenchman, but I married a Scot, Major George Mackenzie (called Mac) and our wedding took place in Germany in 1960. Soon we had two beautiful children, Alexander and Kirsty, both born in Germany, and I enjoyed living the life of a military wife with a batman and many social activities. But in the early 1970s we moved to England and a new life.

We lived in Leicester at first, but soon came down to Torquay where we bought a small hotel before moving to Brixham where we ran a gift shop for a few years. Finally we retired to Paignton where we spent many happy years together until my husband passed away. Since then I have continued to live there on my own and, despite a stroke and heart-attack, I enjoy my craftwork and my writing and spending time with my family. They mean everything to me.

George Mackenzie

Hannelore Mackenzie

Hannelore Mackenzie was born Hannelore Agnes Klara Kaiser in Leipzig, Germany in 1928. She attended school in Magdeburg while the country was in the grip of Hitler's Nazi regime. During World War II she and her family had to struggle to survive. This is the story of that struggle.

Wedding Day
Hannelore, Klara Hannelore's mother, George Mackenzie